▾ ▾ ▾ ▾ ▾ ▾ ▾ ▾ ▾ ▾ ▾ ▾ ▾ ▾ ▾ ▾ ▾ ▾

WHAT WE WISH WE'D KNOWN WHEN WE WERE

NEWLYWEDS

♥ ♥ ♥ ♥ ♥ ♥ ♥ ♥ ♥ ♥ ♥ ♥ ♥ ♥ ♥ ♥ ♥ ♥

WHAT WE WISH WE'D
KNOWN WHEN WE WERE

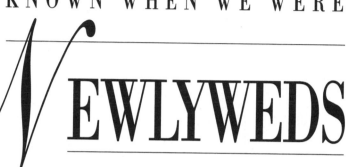

NEWLYWEDS

JOHN & KIMBERLY

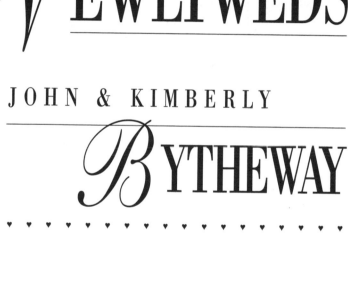

BYTHEWAY

♥ ♥ ♥ ♥ ♥ ♥ ♥ ♥ ♥ ♥ ♥ ♥ ♥ ♥ ♥ ♥ ♥ ♥

BOOKCRAFT

SALT LAKE CITY, UTAH

Library of Congress Cataloging-in-Publication Data

Bytheway, John
  What we wish we'd known when we were newlyweds / John and Kimberly Bytheway.
    p.   cm.
  ISBN 1-57345-649-7 (hc.)
    1. Marriage. 2. Marriage—Religious aspects—Church of Jesus Christ of Latter-Day Saints.   I. Bytheway, Kimberly.
  II. Title.

HQ734.B97 2000
306.81—dc21

                                                            00-023066

Printed in the United States of America   18961-2663B

10   9   8   7   6   5   4   3

To our parents,

Jack and Diane Bytheway

and

Michael and Diane Loveridge

CONTENTS

CHAPTER 1

IS THE HONEYMOON OVER? IT DOESN'T HAVE TO BE . . .

The best way to predict your future is to create it.

–Stephen R. Covey, Quotes and Quips (*Covey Leadership Center, 1993*), p. 52

Congratulations! You've made it through all the years of preparation, all the months of wedding arrangements, and now you're newlyweds! Now that you've finished carrying out those wedding plans, it's time to plan the marriage. Most people will spend a lot of time planning the wedding and then kind of leave the marriage up to chance. That's backwards. The reception didn't come together by itself, and neither will the marriage. Successful marriages don't happen by accident; they take planning and talking and effort. Now that you've returned the tuxedos, and the bridesmaids' dresses are in the backs of their respective closets, real life begins—and it's the best part.

Unfortunately, marriage is not portrayed as a very happy institution in the media these days. *People* magazine and *Entertainment Tonight* tell us which Hollywood couple's marathon four-month marriage broke up this week, while daytime soaps and talk shows present an endless "dysfunction fest." Music on the radio doesn't talk about married love. You don't hear songs that say, "I love my wife so much I think I'll vacuum," or, "I can't wait to see my how my husband likes this meatloaf."

Some people seem to enjoy warning newlyweds that eventually "the honeymoon's over." It makes them feel better to persuade you that once you return from Niagara Falls, real life will hit you in the face like a bug hits a windshield. Maybe you've walked around Food 4 Less and noticed young married couples shopping. Many of them are easy to spot: They're wearing sweats, they looked like they've stopped caring about how they look, and they mope around the store with that "can we afford this?" look on their faces. Even in the Church, if people aren't careful, they may say things like, "Isn't it about time you got married?" making marriage sound more like a chore or a duty than a desirable, wonderful, exciting state.

In light of all this, we'd like to begin with a phrase we didn't hear enough from married couples during our dating and college years. Are you ready? Here it is (please read slowly and with feeling): We *love* being married! It is the greatest. And it seems to get better and better as we work at it. We've been married for a few years now, and we love it even more as it goes along. We even laugh and joke with each other while shopping at Food 4 Less (in nicer attire than sweats, we might add). We think marriage is a blast.

With so many marriages in trouble all around us, we wanted and hoped to hear more people say that kind of thing more often. We wanted to be filled with hope and anticipation about married life, but we didn't hear optimistic statements enough. So we want to say it now—and we hope you'll say it often to young people too—we love being married!

WHY WE WROTE WHAT WE WROTE (SAY THAT TEN TIMES FAST)

When we were engaged, lots of friends approached us and said privately, "Remember, the first year is the hardest, and after that it gets a lot better." We'd smile and look at each other a little puzzled. Looking back now after a few years of marriage, we think they were right. Our first year as a married couple wasn't bad, but it probably was the hardest.

There are many adjustments to make and many expectations that need to be altered when two people come together to create one family. But the important thing is not to get discouraged. Every marriage has adjustments and misunderstandings. It's normal! As you get used to each other, things get easier.

When we sat down to plan this book (actually, we weren't sitting—we were walking around the block with our baby in a stroller), we decided that our main goal was this: *to give young couples tools, ideas, and true principles that will help the first year of marriage go more smoothly.* That's our purpose. We'll give you several ideas that we wish we'd known when we were newlyweds.

4

First we'll talk about the expectations people have for married life, and then we'll talk a little about talking. We'll cover some ways to notice the things your partner does for you, and then we'll put our money where our mouth is and talk about finances in a new marriage. The last chapters will cover intimacy, keeping the romance alive, and involving the Lord in your marriage.

And now, a word about our credentials . . . we don't have any. Except for one: We have a great marriage (right, honey?—nudge, nudge), and we work on improving it all the time. We've also read a ton of marriage books together. Okay, we're exaggerating; we've read ten marriage books together. And we've observed that they all talk about similar important things. There's really nothing new to say about how to have a happy marriage. The hardest part is actually applying the principles you've heard about for years.

Along with our lack of credentials, we're also aware that we are not experts on anything except our own marriage. That's why we called this book "What *We* Wish *We'd* Known When *We* Were Newlyweds." (It wasn't just an attempt to get ten *w*'s in one title.) Hopefully, your marriage and ours will have enough in common that you'll find something helpful in here for you.

One thing that came up again and again as we studied is how many difficulties would be reduced or avoided by simply applying principles of the gospel like faith, patience, and meekness. I guess we should have known. For that reason, we'll share lots of scriptures and counsel from Church leaders.

Well, let's get started on maintaining that marital bliss. May we say again, we love being married. We are committed to our marriage, but we are also committed to marriage as a principle. Marriage is another wonderful evidence of the beauty and wisdom of the plan of salvation.

Is the honeymoon over? We don't think so. Not if you plan your happiness! Can you imagine how much better marriages would be if every couple spent as much time each year planning their marriage as they spent planning their wedding? We think the wonderful, giddy, euphoric, madly-in-love feelings can continue throughout our married years if we create opportunities and plan for them. Sure, there's work and school and bills and budgets and four-for-a-dollar macaroni and cheese. But you don't have to give up being in love. We *refuse* to give up on that! In fact, we're so determined to maintain the marital bliss we felt on our wedding day that we have a little motto in our marriage: "The honeymoon never ends."

ACTION STEPS

THINGS TO DISCUSS:

Do happy marriages take effort?

How long did it take to plan our wedding?

When could we find a regular time to plan our lives?

What kind of marriage do we want to have?

♥

CHAPTER 2

WHAT DID YOU EXPECT?

♥   ♥

There seems to be a superstition among many thousands of our young who hold hands and smooch in the drive-ins that marriage is a cottage surrounded by perpetual hollyhocks to which a perpetually young and handsome husband comes home to a perpetually young and ravishing wife. When the hollyhocks wither and boredom and bills appear the divorce courts are jammed. . . . Anyone who imagines that bliss is normal is going to waste a lot of time running around shouting that he has been robbed.

—Jenkins Lloyd Jones, Deseret News, 12 June 1973, p. A4

What will marriage be like? How did you picture things? Once you leave the altar, your life is truly "altered." It is a *new* life, and you've become a new family. Along with your music tapes and CDs, you each bring a set of expectations into your new marriage, expectations about everything from whose job it is to kill the spiders to who will buy the fabric softener. Some couples think that because they know how to kiss, all their newlywed adjustments will be a piece of cake (or easy as pie, depending on their dessert preferences).

Here's a fictional example of the different expectations a couple might have:

What *She* Expects:

Evenings: I know we'll be tired at the end of the day, but he'll be excited to come home because he only wants to be with me. It will be so nice to be together each night as we eat at a candlelit table, and we'll share our hearts with each other and talk about all of our hopes and dreams and plans.

Showing love: I know he loves me so much that he'll probably shower me with personal gifts or bring flowers every day and write me long love letters.

Talking: I'll really love having someone always there to talk to, and now that we're married I know he'll really open up and talk to me and let me know who he really is inside. I look forward to talking with my new husband each night as he tells me everything about himself. We will just become the best of friends who share everything.

What *He* Expects:

Evenings: When I come home from a long day at work, it'll be fun to have someone I can watch sports with while we eat. Then later I can go play basketball with the elders quorum and not have to worry about calling her every night like I did when we were dating.

Showing love: To show her I love her, I'll make sure the car is always clean and full of gas, I'll make sure she has a flashlight and gloves in the trunk in case anything ever goes wrong, and I'll do home repairs whenever she needs them so she can be comfortable in our new apartment. And I'll work really hard to provide for her.

Talking: It will be nice to come home at the end of the day and just relax and not have to concentrate on being clever or charming. Now I can just be myself.

She'll know I really love her, so I won't have to keep talking. Just being with her will be enough.

Each of these individuals may think his or her set of expectations seems reasonable, even though they're almost opposite from each other. You can see that it's a good idea to talk about how you view your new life together, to clarify your expectations. Talk about a daily routine and about what you expect to do each evening. Talk about how you view your marriage and about the traditions you want to start. We think that the first year goes more smoothly if you talk *a lot!* (This may require hitting the mute button or even—brace yourself—putting down the remote.)

YOUR NEW IDENTITY

While you will always be a member of the family into which you were born, you have now assumed a more important role that must be your first priority. You are now a husband or wife more than anything else. That has to take first place. The scripture says that a man shall "leave his father and his mother, and shall cleave unto his wife" (Genesis 2:24). That goes for a woman too. Elder Hugh B. Brown taught:

> *As each new marriage craft sets sail,*
> *there should be a warning call, which is*
> *familiar to all ocean travelers, "All ashore*
> *that's going ashore," whereupon all in-laws*
> *should get off the matrimonial boat and*
> *return only at infrequent intervals and then*
> *only as invited guests for brief visits.* (You
> and Your Marriage [*Salt Lake City:*
> *Bookcraft, 1960], p. 138*)

If you're fortunate enough to live close to your parents, you are indeed blessed. But you cannot remain as much the son or daughter as you once were without potentially straining your marriage. As for us, we are still very much involved with our families, who are both less than an hour away. We're always careful, however, to check with each other about wanting to join all the family activities. We're a married couple *first,* and our parents' children *second.*

Another reason this separation is important is that there are some things within a marriage that are very personal and shouldn't be shared with extended family members. It's important that both spouses feel emotionally "safe" within the marriage, free to be themselves, even with all their quirks. Spouses need to try to be completely loyal to one another, and not spend every night on the phone telling their parents the latest crazy thing the other one did that wasn't the way their own family used to do it. President Boyd K. Packer expressed it like this:

> *My young sister, you have had some very choice, intimate, cherished times with your mother, talking over things that are sacred and personal. Now all of these moments belong to your husband, and only rarely and on superficial things would you have to run back to mother—maybe for an occasional recipe or a remedy, but on all the sacred and deep and important problems you belong to one another and you solve them between the two of you.* ("Family Togetherness—The Core of the Church," BYU Education Week Devotional Address, *13 June 1963, p. 3*)

Note: All those "recipes and remedies" can really explode a newlywed phone bill! So be brief and call after 5:00 P.M.

If you're like us, you may have to take turns on where you go for Thanksgiving, Christmas, and other occasions. We try to spend a lot of time with both extended families, and in the process we've had to learn to trade off. Merging two day planners into one isn't easy. The important thing is that you talk about it and make sure both of you are happy with the decisions you make. For us, our families live within two miles of each other. Some couples have one set of in-laws an hour away and the other set in Pittsburgh. That situation requires even more sensitivity, because one family will clearly have an advantage. You won't be able to please everyone all the time, so the important thing is that you talk it out, be as fair as possible, and don't let the *blessing* of having an extended family become a source of contention.

WHICH JOB IS YOURS AND WHICH JOB IS MINE?

In a marriage there's always work to be done, but that's nothing new—you had to work when you were single anyway. One fun part of marriage is that you still have all the work, but you're not alone! Of course, life is different after the honeymoon. You're back to school or work, living in an apartment or married student housing or maybe even a house. It's kind of fun! But, as we have learned, whatever you *ob*tain, you have to *main*tain, and there always seems to be work to do. The problem is not the work, but the question: Who does what? This is an important question, and it might be a good topic for your first family home evening.

Perhaps while you were growing up, Dad always took out the garbage. But maybe that was Mom's job in your spouse's house. In some homes Mom did the shopping and Dad balanced the checkbook and paid the bills. Maybe Mom cooked and Dad did the dishes.

It's a good idea to decide how you will do things. Some couples never talk about these everyday chores; they just "expect" their spouse to do something because that's the way it was when they were growing up. A young wife shared this experience with us:

> *Growing up, my dad always hung the*
> *Christmas lights, so naturally when I was*

♥ *first married, I expected my husband to do the same. As Thanksgiving came and went, and Christmas drew closer, I waited and waited, but my husband never attempted to even look for our box of lights. As the days grew into weeks, I grew more and more impatient. I even went to the attic and set the lights on the stairs as a "gentle hint" that he needed to get out there and make our roof and bushes look festive. I found myself getting angrier and angrier as night after night I came home and saw the box sitting exactly where I had left it long before—untouched. It certainly tainted the spirit of the season, and the spirit of our marriage. Finally, one evening, I just asked him if he would hang the lights, and the next afternoon it was done. How much energy I had wasted on anger and impatience when all we needed to do was talk about our expectations earlier.* ♥

At our house, John is the garbage man. He keeps the wastebaskets from overflowing, and he takes that big-black-thing-with-wheels to the curb each Friday. Kim likes to do the shopping, so her job is to keep the fridge full. We made a deal that if Kim would do the cooking, John would do the dishes. You may need to make a few deals too. Here's a list of some of the other routine chores at our place.

Laundry

Ironing

Dishes

Cars (getting gas, changing the oil, washing, and vacuuming)

Dusting

Vacuuming

Cooking

Cleaning

Yard (mowing, weeding, gardening)

Budgeting, checkbook balancing

Family home evening

Family scripture study

Family prayer

Maybe these duties will kind of fall into place with the passing of time, but it's still a good idea to talk often about your expectations, because if one of you starts feeling as if you're doing most of the work, you might begin to feel unappreciated. No one wants to feel that way. A wonderful way of making sure your partner feels okay about the duty roster is to ask on occasion, "Do you feel like I'm doing enough?" In our own marriage, although we have things fairly neatly divided between us, as a general rule we always help out the other when we can.

LOOKS AREN'T EVERYTHING, BUT THEY'RE SOMETHING

John Says:

When I was in college, I noticed a funny cartoon on the refrigerator of one of the girls in my student ward. It showed a bride running down the aisle after the marriage ceremony, shouting, "Hooray, no more diets, no more makeup!" The groom was watching her with an alarmed look on his face, wondering if he'd just made a mistake.

It's a wonderful feeling to be proud of your spouse. For the first part of our marriage, Kim spent a few weeks working on thank-you notes for wedding gifts. It was a lot of work. But even though she was in the house all day, she still took care of herself by putting on her makeup and doing her hair. She wanted to look good for her husband when he came home. (And her husband appreciated it!)

Husbands should not expect their wives to look great if they're content to hang around the house unshowered, unshaved, and undeodoranted. (Is that a word?)

Continuing to care about your appearance is important. It may be that one of the reasons your spouse fell in love with you in the first place was because you were attractive and took such good care of yourself. You wouldn't want to deprive your spouse of one of the things that drew him or her to you when you were dating, would you? Also, what kind of a message does it send to your spouse if you stop caring about how you look? "Well, we're married now and my spouse will have to accept me no matter what." Don't let the beginning of marriage be the end of hygiene.

Another benefit of marriage is having a full-time fashion consultant available when you're going to a wedding reception or to church. We always try to dress in the attire our spouse likes best. (We're careful not to use the old, "You're not going to wear *that*, are you?" line.)

TV OR NOT TV?

The television can be a source of contention if it gets more quality time than the marriage. The problem is, television watching inhibits conversation, and conversation is vital to a marriage. Some couples get in the habit of watching TV while they eat, thus losing one of the best opportunities for conversation: dinnertime.

It may be that the two of you enjoy watching sports or Captain Picard together, and that's okay. It becomes a problem, however, when one of you wants or needs to talk, and the other is, well, spaced out, warped, or waiting for halftime. It's funny, but a wife might complain that her husband spends too much time watching TV when he truly feels like he hardly watches at all. Again, the important thing is that you talk about your expectations, be willing to compromise, and come to an agreement. That's where the communication comes in. It isn't that one of you is right and the other is wrong, it's that you *feel* differently, and that's where the trouble starts. Especially in the first year of marriage, it's critical to try to understand one another's needs. She may need more time alone together, and he may need more time to relax and unwind.

IS THAT A BYTHEWAY THING OR A LOVERIDGE THING?

Different families do things differently. We remember once when we were loading the dishwasher together. John was putting the spoons and forks in right side up, and Kim was putting them in upside down. When we noticed the difference, one of us said, "I've always put them in this way. Is that a Bytheway thing?" or "Is that a Loveridge thing?" (Loveridge is Kim's maiden name.)

We've used those sentences millions of times since then. We do many things a certain way because that's how our families did them. When one of us sees the other doing something differently from the way we do it, we ask about it so we can find out if theirs is a *better* way or just a *different* way that doesn't really make much difference. Most of the time, we find that it doesn't really matter. In fact, when John loads the dishwasher, he still puts the silverware in right side up, and Kim still loads it upside down. It doesn't matter to us. What *does* matter is keeping the Spirit in our marriage, and keeping contention out. We would much rather have different silverware loading methods, with the Spirit, than have one spouse mandate "the true and living silverware loading method," and have contention in our home. We've also learned that the sentence "I've always done it this way" is a lot better than the tactless "That's not the way to do it. You're doing it wrong."

DON'T EXPECT EXACT CHANGE

Some couples go into marriage expecting that they can change their spouses into exactly what they want. Soon enough, everyone learns that the people who walk out of the sealing room are the same ones who walked in. Marriage, by itself, doesn't change people. Elder Hugh W. Pinnock taught:

> *You must ever realize that you had better marry the person who has the built in characteristics you desire because marriage is not a place where you will be able to change another to fit him or her into the mold of what you want.* ("Ten Keys to Successful Dating and Marriage Relationships," BYU Fireside and Devotional Speeches, *1981, pp. 70–71)*

WHAT WE WISH WE'D KNOWN WHEN WE WERE *Newlyweds*

On that happy note, let's emphasize another principle. Rather than expecting change, focus mostly on what you don't want to change. Focus on the positive things, the things that brought you together and helped you fall in love. We know an older couple who have a delightful marriage, and on their wedding day, the new husband said, "There's 80 percent of me that's good, and there's about 20 percent of me that's not so good. If you focus on the 20 percent, we'll have problems, but if you focus on the 80 percent, we'll be fine."

One of our favorite stories that has helped us in our marriage is about a woman who read in a magazine that spouses should sit down together and talk about the little things that annoy them about each other. She dutifully assembled a list and prepared to explain each item to her husband.

Her first complaint was with the way he ate grapefruit, peeling it like an orange instead of cutting it in half and sectioning it. This drove her crazy! And she went on down her list. Then it was his turn. She describes what happened next:

> *Though it has been more than half a*
> *century, I still carry a mental image of my*

husband's handsome young face as he gath-
ered his brows together in a thoughtful,
puzzled frown and then looked at me with
his large eyes and said, "Well, to tell the
truth, I can't think of anything I don't like
about you, Honey."

Can you imagine how that made her feel? She real-
ized she had been finding fault with trivial things like
how he ate grapefruit, while he had been ignoring or
choosing not to worry about the little things she did that
might have been annoying. She concludes:

I wish I could say that this experience
completely cured me of fault finding. It
didn't. But it did make me aware early in
my marriage that husbands and wives need
to keep in perspective, and usually ignore,
the small differences in their habits and per-
sonalities. Whenever I hear of married
couples being incompatible, I always won-
der if they are suffering from what I now
call the Grapefruit Syndrome. (Lola B.
Walters, Ensign, April 1993, p. 13)

We have adopted Sister Walters's phrase, "Grapefruit Syndrome," and it has helped us to put each other's little quirks into perspective.

EXPECT YOUR LOVE TO GROW

Your first year of marriage might not be exactly what you expected, but that just makes life more interesting. One of the fun things about marriage is discovering how different people do different things, and finding that you can enjoy and value the differences. You might even learn a few better ways of doing things. Having harmony in your marriage doesn't come from being exactly the same. That would be called melody. *Harmony* is being different, together. Lesson number one for us was that marriage is humbling. If you approach yours with humility, you'll learn a lot.

So what if your husband doesn't come home on a white horse—you can get used to a green Corolla. And so what if your wife doesn't dress like a model—that's okay, your budget will do better at Wal-Mart anyway. Focus on what you've got and expect your love to grow. We expect it will.

ACTION STEPS

THINGS TO DISCUSS:

> How did you picture married life?
>
> How do you imagine a typical day of married life?
>
> What kind of work would you like to do around the house?
>
> How can I be the kind of spouse you want?

RECOMMENDED READING:

> Brent A. Barlow, *What Wives Expect of Husbands* (Salt Lake City: Deseret Book, 1982)
>
> Brent A. Barlow, *What Husbands Expect of Wives* (Salt Lake City: Deseret Book, 1983)

CHAPTER 3

CAN WE TALK?

♥ ♥

Marriages are not successful merely because these couples have fewer problems than others, but they are successful because, when problems come, as come they will, a husband and wife sit down together to solve their problems like grown-up, mature individuals, rather than with the immaturity of adolescence.

—Teachings of Harold B. Lee, ed. Clyde J. Williams (Salt Lake City: Bookcraft, 1996), p. 248

One day, an old friend approached John and asked, "What is the number one thing you've learned from your first year of marriage?" John replied, "To keep my mouth shut!" At first, this response may sound a little negative, but the implication is that if you keep your mouth *shut*, you might just have your ears *open*. As a wise person once said, "The way to save face is to leave the lower half tightly shut." We've learned that effective communication is as much about listening as it is about talking.

HERE'S THE POINT—SOMETIMES THERE DOESN'T HAVE TO BE A POINT

We have also learned that men and women talk for different reasons. Generally speaking, *men talk for information, but women talk for interaction* (see Deborah Tannen, *You Just Don't Understand* [New York: Ballantine Books, 1990], p. 81). That concept has saved us a lot of frustration.

Before we understood that idea, we had experiences like these: Sometimes John would stop by his parents' home, and his mother would begin to tell him everything about all his other siblings and what they were doing, right down to each niece and nephew. John knows how to listen, but in the back of his mind he was thinking, "There must be something in here I need to *know*." Finally, he'd say, "Mom, what's the point?" You see, John was listening for information, but his mom wasn't talking to give *information*, she was talking to enjoy the *interaction*. Mom would respond, "Point? What point? Why does there have to be a point? This is a conversation, not a hearing! We're a family, so we talk!"

When Kim and her mom and sisters get together, it takes an act of Congress to get them apart. They talk for hours, as if there were no such thing as time. They share *everything*, not because they have several crucial points to make from their outline, but because they love to interact, to express feelings, to empathize and support each other.

Men interact too, but it's different. When John goes home to see "the fam," he and his dad and all his brothers might watch a ball game together. Mom and the sisters are more likely to go in the front room and "visit." Men will usually bond around an activity, like golf or woodworking or watching sports. Women will usually bond by talking. If we can understand these differences, our listening will improve, and therefore our communication will be more effective.

I'M NOT BROKEN, SO DON'T FIX ME

Kim Says:

One of John's jobs around the house is to notice broken things and fix them. He does repairs on the car, fiddles with the computer, and completes any number of little mechanical jobs. He never seems happier than when he's packing his Black and Decker cordless drill/screwdriver around looking for broken things.

Is it any wonder, then, that when I want to talk, John (like most men) listens with the intent to "fix"? He's got all his mental power tools charged and ready for action. But here's the problem: I don't want to be fixed. I'm not broken! I'm not asking for solutions; I just want a listening ear.

Generally speaking, when a woman hears another woman describe a problem, she might empathize by saying, "Wow, I know how you feel. Something similar happened to me once . . ." A man hearing the same problem might, with the motive of sincerely trying to help, say, "Well, have you tried this?" Or he might even think that he can help the situation by reducing or minimizing the problem: "Oh, that sort of thing happens all the time; I wouldn't even worry about it." Even though his motives might be sincere, he's not helping. He might even be hurting, because what his wife actually hears is something like, "You have no reason to feel like that—those are stupid feelings to have."

So what do you do? You value the differences, and you try to understand the other person's *reason* for talking. Husbands can concentrate on listening to feelings and take some time each day to "just talk." To your wife, *what* you talk about is not nearly as important as the fact that you're talking. Wives can take it as a compliment when they're invited to a ball game to "bond." If you're just trying to vent your feelings, you can gently remind your husband, "I want to talk to you, and I don't really want advice right now, I just want you to know what I'm feeling." Even if you do these things clumsily, the fact that you're trying will send a strong message of love and commitment. As the saying goes, "Bumbling love is better than carefully executed indifference."

FEELINGS BEFORE FACTS

One time, while reading the Book of Mormon, we noticed that perhaps Father Lehi knew all about this idea of listening to understand. Sariah was worried about her sons, who had returned to Jerusalem to get the brass plates from a man who didn't want to give them up. She was understandably concerned. One day, Sariah told Lehi her feelings. He didn't jump immediately to a solution, but let his wife get all her feelings out first.

Nephi reports, "She . . . complained against my father, telling him that he was a visionary man; saying: Behold thou hast led us forth from the land of our inheritance, and my sons are no more, and we perish in the wilderness" (1 Nephi 5:2). Lehi's response was perfect. He didn't say, "Behold, how dare you!" He didn't say, "Why are you worried about that?" And he certainly didn't tell her that she was wrong. Instead, he *agreed* with her and supported her in her feelings. He said, "I know that I am a visionary man" (1 Nephi 5:4). Brilliant! What a perfect response. Then he explained his own feelings. We call this response "feelings before facts," or "listen before logic." (Fortunately the boys showed up with the brass plates a few verses later.) Are we reading more into this episode than is really there? Perhaps. But the principle is sound, and it has helped us in our marriage. Listen past the words for the feelings and respond to them first.

ACTIONS SPEAK LOUDER

Imagine a new husband on his way home from work or school. In his mind he's expecting an excited hug-and-kiss welcome from his wife. Finally he opens the front door and, voilà! His wife's on the phone. She gestures a wave and keeps talking. That's okay; she'll end the call quickly now that he's come home. Five minutes pass, then ten minutes, then fifteen. She's still talking about something that happened in high school and she hasn't said once, "My husband just got home, I have to go." What do the actions say? *This phone call is more important than you.* She hasn't said a word, but her actions are unmistakable.

Listening is an action that sends a message. This is another reason why listening is so powerful. It says, "You are important to me." It says, "I have time for you." It says, "Your feelings are important to me." Listening while watching TV or reading the paper, on the other hand, says, "This paper or TV show is most important to me,

but you can supply some background noise if you wish."
Dr. Brent Barlow writes:

> *While many men are physically present in the home, they are often psychologically absent. Too many husbands bring home unfinished work or spend a disproportionate amount of time working at hobbies, reading newspapers, taking catnaps, or watching television. A husband's physical presence in the home should be matched by his psychological presence. Wives don't like to be ignored, particularly when husbands are at home.* (What Wives Expect of Husbands *[Salt Lake City: Deseret Book, 1982], p. 128)*

John Says:

One day, after I finished a class at school, I walked out to the truck and found a paper sack on the seat. Along with a dozen frosted cookies, there was a note inside that said, "Welcome to the Twelve Days of Valentine's." Each day for twelve days I received a little gift or treat and a card. Every day after work I looked forward to going back to the truck! I saved every one of those little notes (husbands, take note—save every note your wife writes to you), but the actions spoke louder than the words.

First of all, Kim found the truck among thousands of cars on campus. That alone is no small feat. She also worked over a hot stove making cookies. I can't remember all the words on those twelve cards. But I remember the actions. The actions said, "I love you, I love you, I love you, I love you," for twelve days in a row. To paraphrase the book of James, "Show me your love without your works, and I'll show you my love by my works."

Kim Says:

One time, driving home from Idaho, John did something brilliant. It had been a long day, and we were anxious to get home. In the rush of everything, I had felt a little neglected. It was already dark, and we had a four-hour drive ahead of us. As we passed through Idaho Falls, John had a prompting. Whether it was the voice of conscience, intuition, or the Spirit, he's not sure. But he thought to himself, "Pull the car over and give your wife a hug." At this point, John asked, "What for?" But the prompting returned. So, although we were in a hurry, John pulled the car over, pulled me close, and gave me a hug. No words were spoken, and he didn't look at his watch and ask, "I wonder how long I have to hug her for it to count," he just held me close for probably half a minute. Then, without a word, he sat back, restarted the car, and resumed the journey. A few miles down the road, I said, "You have no idea how much I needed that." John later told me he wanted to reach up and high-five whoever put that thought in his head. Since that experience, we've tried, even when there is no prompting, to pull each other close from time to time, just to embrace.

It's a good idea to focus not only on what you say in your marriage but on what your actions say. When schedules are busy and you don't get to see each other much, make sure when you're together that you use actions and words to show your commitment.

I DIDN'T MEAN TO

Sometimes we hurt each other's feelings without meaning to. When two people get together from different families and backgrounds and try to live together, that's inevitable. Early in our marriage, we came to an understanding that has helped us a great deal: We promised that we would never *intentionally* hurt each other's feelings, and then we promised that if we ever did

feel hurt, we would remind ourselves of that commitment.

Today, if one of us is bugged by something the other
person did or said, we remember that we have an agreement, and that the offense wasn't on purpose. Just know-
ing that helps a lot. Then we take the next step and talk
it out so that we won't repeat it. This way Kim knows
that if John did something insensitive, it wasn't on purpose, and John knows that if Kim did something that
made him feel "second place," it wasn't her intention to
do so. Then, when we get to the point that we can talk
about it, we remind each other, "You know I would never
intentionally do that!" and we try to make changes to
avoid the problem in the future.

It takes a lot of mental discipline to remind yourself
that your spouse really wouldn't do anything to hurt you
on purpose. It can be so easy to get offended unless you
remind yourself that you are *both* trying to make a happy
marriage, and that neither of you really wants a hurt or
angry spouse. You may find, too, that when you try to
overlook the little things *before* you get offended, you can
avoid a lot of problems. So much of what offends people

is small stuff. If you're mature enough to marry, you're mature enough to overlook the fact that someone put the toilet paper on the dispenser backward. This way you can avoid the hurt altogether.

For some, just the thought of getting into one of those "discussions" about problems is too frightening. At first, we found that talking didn't come as naturally as it does today. Sometimes it just takes time—and we don't mean a few minutes or even a few hours. There is something about being together for months and months, and even years, that makes the communication come easier. It can be discouraging when your spouse would rather sulk in the bathroom than talk to you, but rest assured that in time, as you build trust, talking through your problems will come more naturally.

POWER TOOLS FOR COMMUNICATING

Have you ever heard of the "paradox of Abilene"? The paradox of Abilene is that there are a lot of people living for no apparent reason in this place where no one would ever want to be. (Actually, John has been to Abilene, and he liked it.) If you haven't heard of the paradox, then perhaps you've heard of the proverbial "trip to Abilene." That's when you both end up going where neither one of you wanted to go because you each thought the *other* person wanted to. "Do you want to go bowling?" "Sure. Do you?" "Yeah, that's fine." So off you go, only to find out later that you both would rather have stayed home and watched a movie.

We'd like to share a couple of tools that have helped us immensely in this aspect of our marriage. When we're trying to make a decision together about what we should do, we use the number rating system. We learned this from Brother Douglas Brinley's audiocassette presentation *Marital Relationships Seminar*, which we highly recommend.

This is how it works: Let's say we're trying to decide what to do for our Friday date night. One of us might say, "Do you want to see a movie tonight?" Instead of choosing between "yes" or "no," we use the rating system. John might say, "Oh, I'm about a four on that one," and Kim might say, "I'm about a six." Which means we'll start all over again and come up with another idea that we both give a higher rating.

The rating system helps us communicate what we really want without having to guess about our partner. This way we don't end up doing things together that neither one of us really wants to do!

Kim Says:

Another tool we use came from my college friends. When they wanted to make sure someone was telling the truth, instead of saying, "really?" they would say, "*sternfalter?*" As far as we know, that's not really a word, but it is to us. Sometimes I will say, "John, do you mind if I take the car and go visit my mom today while you're working?" And John will say, "No, that's okay, just buckle up and be safe." If I'm not sure how John really feels, I'll say, "Is it okay then, *sternfalter?*" That's John's cue to say what he *really* thinks. Again, we had to make a deal on this one. We've promised we'll always tell what we really feel when the truth-serum word *sternfalter* is used. So John might respond, "Really, *sternfalter*, you go ahead, and I'll work on this . . ." It might sound strange, but this little word has helped us get to the other person's true feelings—*sternfalter*, it has.

Here's a little note of caution. Although we believe in being honest, that doesn't mean it's necessary to tell each other about *everything*. For example, we would never use the *sternfalter* word to get information on other subjects that might be painful or uncomfortable. We use it only when we want to make sure what we're doing is okay with our spouse. These two communication tools, the rating system and *sternfalter,* have helped our communication, and we hope they will help yours too.

TALKING ABOUT PROBLEMS, OR WHEN "NOTHING" MEANS "SOMETHING"

If you're like every other normal couple, you will encounter problems and misunderstandings and hurt feelings in your first year. Don't let it get you down! It's normal, and it's not permanent. But it's critical that you talk about these things with your spouse. Stephen Covey has written, "Unexpressed feelings don't die. They are buried alive and come forth later in uglier ways. People who over and over again take the martyr role gradually build internal resentments and hostilities which eventually surface" (Truman G. Madsen and Stephen R. Covey, *Marriage and Family: Gospel Insights* [Salt Lake City: Bookcraft, 1983], p. 175).

Marriage is humbling. No one wants to be told, "You did this wrong, and you did this wrong." But it is critical in this first year that both partners try to listen and understand. The way you react now will determine whether your spouse will be willing to bring things up again in the future. And it would be a great comfort to both of you if you knew that your marriage had an "open door, open mind" policy. On the other hand, if you react with resentment during one of these chats, your partner may say, "I'm never bringing anything up again," and then you've got a worse problem.

We believe that, more important than all the communication techniques we could share, the main thing you need is simply the willingness to listen. That willingness to talk about problems, to look at them honestly and try to solve them, might be called meekness. Remember that when Jesus said to the apostles, "one of you shall betray me," they all asked, "Is it I?" (Matthew 26:21–22). That kind of meekness and introspection will help you as you encounter these speed bumps on the road to marital bliss. If your spouse seems to feel betrayed, you might ask, "Is it I?" or, "Is it something I did?"

Most of us have different ways of dealing with problems. Some will clam up and disappear emotionally and even physically. Some might want to talk right away and figure out what's wrong. Some might be tempted just to bury a problem and try to forget it because it's late and they don't have time or energy for a "talk." Finding a method that both of you agree on takes time.

When you know there's a problem, what do you do? One spouse might sense that something's up and ask, "What's wrong?" Sometimes, the response isn't very helpful: "Nothing," which may be followed by silence, which usually means, "Something." Sometimes people need time alone to "process" their feelings, and that's fine. If that's the case for you, and you want to be alone for a while to figure things out, it's really helpful to say something like, "I'm willing to talk about it, but I just need some time right now." That's a much better, kinder answer than "Nothing."

Some spouses might want to sentence their partners to a different kind of MTC, the "Marriage Torture Chamber." This is the "Well, if you don't know what's wrong, I'm not going to tell you" method. "If you're so insensitive that you don't know what you did, I'll just let you worry and stew about it until you figure it out." We would call this approach "punishing insensitivity by being insensitive."

You can't expect your spouse to be a genius in ESP. If your partner doesn't know what's wrong, sulking around and giving the silent treatment won't help him or her figure it out. For some reason, some spouses have the idea that "if my partner really loves me, he'll know (or she'll know) what's wrong." But being married doesn't give a person the power of a mind reader. Until we learn sci-fi movie telepathy, we might have to fall back to the good old-fashioned method of communication called *talking*.

When it *is* time to talk, a little diplomacy is always nice. This is why some spouses might say, "I need some time before we talk," so they can figure out *how* they want to express their feelings. The goal is to say things in the kindest and gentlest way, not to come out with guns blazing. Remember, you will eventually "kiss and make up," but if there were any harsh words spoken, *they* will be remembered. Being overly critical probably hurts more than it helps. We doubt that anyone is ever criticized into changing. On the other hand, many people have been loved into changing.

We've found that it's better to talk about a person's actions rather than the person. For example, rather than saying, "You are so rude," you might say, "When you said I smelled like a yak in summer, it made me feel bad. Can you see why that hurt my feelings a little?" (An extreme example, we hope.) Some couples will hold hands when they have these little chats. We recommend it. It's hard to be mad at someone when you're holding that person's hand.

Discussion time is when the listening part of communication becomes really vital. That is why John said the most important thing he learned in the first year was to "keep his mouth shut." It may be very tempting to interrupt and say, "yeah, but . . ." or even to take issue with your spouse's argument or how he or she remembers the facts. However, you will communicate more effectively if you try to truly understand the other person before you respond. When someone is describing feelings, it is best to let the person get it all out before dealing with the particulars. You have to let off steam before you can cool down. Once the feelings are all out, and your partner is still there (holding your hand), you can start dealing with the problem. This is another example of the "feelings before facts" idea discussed earlier.

Remember that feelings aren't right or wrong, they're just feelings. Saying "It's wrong to feel like that" isn't helpful. If people feel hurt, they feel hurt. It may be that they misunderstood something, or don't have all the facts, but for the time being, their feelings need to be acknowledged, not dismissed.

We have found that when one of us says, "When you did this, it made me feel like this," we discover things that may not have occurred to us. It wasn't that we were being purposely insensitive, it's just that we didn't think about how something we said or did would be perceived by our partner. This is when we have to remember the "If I ever hurt you, please understand it wasn't intentional" deal we made earlier.

As we've been writing about this, we've thought of all the "crisis talks" we've had, and the funny thing is, we can't seem to remember what they were about! What we *do* remember, however, is the tone or spirit of those discussions. That's why it's important to be kind and loving in your choice of words. If you use hurtful or accusing words, the day will come when you can't remember what the argument was about, but you might still remember the awful things that were said!

Many times before we had one of these chats, we each said a silent prayer. (We didn't know it at the time, but we discovered later that we had both prayed first.) If the spirit of faith and charity and repentance can be at work, then the Lord is part of your marriage, and these little chats can end with the two of you feeling even closer than before.

Although we consider our marriage to be very strong, we had many of these "crisis talks" in our first year. Perhaps our marriage works *because* we had so many of these chats. They may take a lot of time, but they're worth the investment. Again, they won't be as frequent as time goes on, so don't get discouraged. The fact that they come up doesn't mean you have a bad marriage.

We've heard that an airliner flying to a far-off destination is off course *most* of the time! The pilot is constantly making little course corrections along the way so the airplane eventually arrives at its destination. Newlywed life might be like that too—you may need to make many course corrections in the first year. That's okay; they're necessary to keep you heading in the right direction.

TWO EARS, NO WAITING

Some couples talk deeply only when there are problems, and that's unfortunate. We've heard of wives who force themselves to cry because it's the only way they can get their husbands to pay attention to them. That's a crying shame. In our marriage, we've really tried to keep the communication lines open by spending a lot of time talking and listening. Sometimes, when we're driving, we'll turn off the radio and just gab. We've created some of our best memories talking and laughing together in the car. We believe that talking helps us grow together, while silence might make us grow apart. Husband-and-wife communication is an art. It's something that will improve as you work at it.

ACTION STEPS

THINGS TO DISCUSS:

Do you keep problems to yourself, or do you like to get
them out quickly?

Do you think you talk more for information or for interaction?

How can I best respond to you when you have a problem?

RECOMMENDED READING:

Douglas R. Brinley, *Marital Relationships Seminar,* audiocassette presentation (Salt Lake City: Covenant
Communications, 1988)

Deborah Tannen, *You Just Don't Understand* (New York:
Ballantine Books, 1990)

CHAPTER 4

YOU NOTICED! EXPRESSING APPRECIATION

♥ ——————————————————————— ♥

If you want to sacrifice the admiration of many men for
the criticism of one, go ahead, get married.

—Katharine Hepburn

During dating and courtship, many people put their
future spouses on a pedestal and think of them as ideal in
every way. People are rarely critical to their fiancés.
Within a marriage, however, they see more of the imper-
fections in their partners. Certainly after the wedding day
people "come down to earth," but that doesn't mean they

should treat their spouses like dirt. No one gets married just so they can have someone always there to remind them of their faults.

How does your spouse want to be treated? That's a very wise question for a newlywed to ask. We believe that what most women want, more than anything else, is to be *cherished* by their husbands. Or, more accurately, they want to *feel* cherished by their husbands, and that comes through not only in words but in a multitude of little actions. We believe that what most men want from their wives is to be *admired*, to be looked up to, and to be loved. This also comes down to daily actions and words. We believe that one of the best questions you can ask your spouse on a daily basis is, "What can I do for you today to let you know that I love you?"

Some wives might appreciate flowers. Some might want help with the house. Some might prefer some conversation. Husbands, on the other hand, may prefer physical touch over gifts. That's why it's important to ask. Dr. Gary Chapman, author of *The Five Love Languages* (Chicago: Northfield Publishers, 1995), identifies the following five ways of expressing love:

1. Quality time

2. Words of affirmation

3. Gifts

4. Acts of service

5. Physical touch

He suggests that every person has a "primary love language," or the one he or she prefers most.

Have you ever been eager to show your love to your partner, only to find that your efforts seem to fall flat? Maybe you haven't found out which "love language" your spouse desires the most. A husband might come home and want to take his wife out to dinner to get her away from the house, when what she would really prefer is having him help with laundry or vacuuming or dusting.

John Says:

I used to think that keeping cars clean and running smoothly sent a powerful "I love you." I have learned that, although auto maintenance is greatly appreciated, Kim prefers vegetation and words (flowers and notes). My opinion of flowers is that they're very pretty at first, but in three days they're dead. But what *I* think is not important in this case. If I want to say "I love you" in Kim's language, colorful and aromatic flora is the way.

NOTICING VERSUS NAGGING

We've all heard the saying that "behind every good man is a good woman" (and the alternate version, "Behind every good man is a surprised woman"). Some may believe that their job is to help their spouses become more than they are, and that's true. But what may be intended as encouragement for the future can sound like complaining in the present. For example, if a wife is constantly telling her husband all that he "could" be doing, or all that he "should" be doing, she may sincerely believe she's being the "good woman" pushing her husband to greater heights. However, the husband may begin to think, "No matter what I do, it's not good enough," or, "When we were dating, she used to say I was wonderful, and that made me want to be with her. Now she's always complaining and telling me I should be doing more, which makes me want to be somewhere else."

Again, what most men want in marriage is to be admired and appreciated. Certainly there should be encouragement for the future, but when a wife praises her husband for *present* blessings and accomplishments, the husband will be motivated from within to do more because he wants to please his loving and supportive wife.

President Ezra Taft Benson taught, "[Pride] is manifest in so many ways, such as faultfinding, gossiping, back-biting, murmuring, living beyond our means, envying, coveting, *withholding gratitude and praise that might lift another,* and being unforgiving and jealous" (*Ensign,* May 1989, p. 5; emphasis added). So when it comes to grati-tude and praise for the present, don't hold back!

Elder Joe J. Christensen has written: "There is great meaning in the statement by Robert Bierstedt: 'It isn't what *I* think of me, and it isn't what *you* think of me, but it is what I *think* you think of me.' We tend to be painfully aware of our weaknesses—most of us don't need frequent reminders. Few people have ever changed for the better as a result of constant nagging. If we are not careful, some of what we offer as constructive criticism is actually destructive. At times, it is better to leave some things unsaid" (*One Step at a Time* [Salt Lake City: Deseret Book, 1996], p. 24).

We believe that noticing the positive things is a pow-erful habit to develop in the first year of marriage. From time to time, a bit of encouragement for the future from our partner is appreciated, but never as much as when we are reminded that we are doing a good job in the present.

Kim Says:

Early in our first year, I decided to make my first pot roast for dinner. I even called my mom to get that special blend of spices that would make it extra tantalizing. Well, I figured that if a little is good, a lot must be even better, and I went wild with the oregano and steak seasoning. That night, after the meat had simmered for more than six hours, I was so anxious to present this feast of a lifetime to my husband. One bite later, I knew immediately my mistake in presuming that "more was more" (perhaps with spices, *less* is always more). I was so embarrassed, but one comment from John let me know that I had married the right man. He simply said, "Thank you for working so hard all day to make us this nice dinner." Note that he didn't say "delicious." But it didn't matter. He *noticed* that it had taken a lot of preparation for me to put that meal on the table, and although it hadn't turned out the way either of us had expected, it was all right. John wanted a happy wife more than a satisfied stomach. It goes back to noticing that 80 percent good part we talked

about earlier, and well, only about 80 percent of my meals are worth eating, but that's the part that John focuses on.

It makes all the difference in a marriage to be appreciated for the little things that you do. It is easy when your wife cleans the sinks to point out that she forgot to shine the fixtures. When your husband unloads the dishwasher, you might wince over the fact that he put the glasses in the wrong cupboard. But if you ever want him to unload the dishwasher again, it's a good idea to overlook the thorns and point out the roses.

We talked earlier about the division of labor in your new house or apartment, but it should never be so rigid that you can't help with each other's jobs. At our house, Kim usually takes the responsibility of vacuuming the floor, but sometimes John is the one running the Hoover. (John wishes they would design a riding vacuum cleaner.) This sends two different messages: (1) that he appreciates the other things Kim is busy with so he helps out, and (2) that he recognizes that vacuuming can be monotonous, and so he takes a turn now and again. He doesn't always verbally express his appreciation, but it is obvious through his actions.

Admittedly, though, sometimes those little acts of service go unnoticed in the hustle and bustle of everyday life. We like to point out to each other what we did, then do the ol' "big toe in the sand" routine and say things like, "Aw, shucks, it was nothing." Sometimes we make it a game, saying, "See if you can find what home repair I did in the living room today," or, "Does anything look different to you?" (For added suspense, whistle the music to *Jeopardy* as your spouse looks for your act of service.)

WORDS THAT STICK

We think words are nice. In fact, we think they are essential. From the first days of our marriage, we have made it a habit to leave little notes all around our house for each other to discover. (We believe sticky notes were invented for this lofty purpose.) We often leave love notes, but we also take time to express a few words of appreciation for something that our spouse did. It might just be "Thanks for being my wife" or "This sink belongs in the porcelain hall of fame." That's all it takes, just a few seconds, a few words, stuck in a conspicuous place, and it makes a world of difference.

Like Old Faithful at Yellowstone, we like to "gush and flow." You know how disappointing it can be when you have worked hard on something for someone else, and the only response is, "Oh, yeah, that's nice." It takes all the wind out of your sails and reduces your motivation for going above and beyond the duty roster in the future. So after we point out these "anonymous" acts of service we've done for each other, we say, "Yeah, it does look nice, doesn't it? Go ahead, gush and flow." It's funny, but when you know that someone will notice a job you've done, you make an extra effort to make sure to do it well.

♥   ♥

IF THE SHOE DOESN'T FIT, PUT YOURSELF IN IT

A word to husbands: As you come home from school or work, you might stay in the car for a minute and think about your wife's shoes. What would it be like to be in them? What has she been doing all day? What are the first words you will say when you walk in? What would make her feel cherished and missed? She may be excited to tell or show you something, so your first words will be important. After shifting from Drive into Park, shift one more gear in your head, and remember your role as a husband. Harold B. Lee taught:

> *May you young husbands realize that the home is your wife's castle where from morning till night she toils to build in that home a lovely shrine at which her husband and her children might worship. For you to fail to appreciate her efforts or to disregard the sanctity of her home and its orderliness by your careless habits, would be to put into her mind the dangerous thought that her husband doesn't appreciate her efforts.* (Decisions for Successful Living [Salt Lake City: Deseret Book, 1973], p. 178)

And now, a word to the wives: You can make a similar effort by imagining what your husband has been up to all day. What's going on in his shoes (besides athlete's foot)? What might make him feel admired and loved? What words would he love to hear from his wife at the end of the day? "Did you wipe your feet?" probably isn't the breath of fresh air he expected, is it? Harold B. Lee also said:

> *You young wives must realize that as
> your companion comes home from his day's
> labor, he comes sometimes with nerves that
> are taut with the tensions of that day's
> efforts, hoping to find in you someone to
> give him the strength and the courage to go
> back inspired and better prepared to meet
> the problems of the next day. To nag and to
> scold and to fail to appreciate his problems is
> to fail in being the companion that he needs.*
> (Decisions for Successful Living, p. 178)

♥   ♥

William James wrote, "The deepest principle of human nature is the craving to be appreciated." Make it your goal never to become so used to marriage that you fail to notice all the little things your spouse does for you.

There is a lot of work in the first year of marriage. There may be school for both husband and wife, possibly with growing debt, along with job responsibilities and tough decisions to make. That's a tremendous amount of pressure. Just remember how many times you've heard older couples comment on how they struggled financially when they were newly married, and yet how wonderful those first years were. If your first years are filled with struggle, make sure they are also filled with faith and appreciation.

ACTION STEPS

THINGS TO DISCUSS:

How can I best show my love for you? Do you like gifts? notes? touch? time? service?

What help could I give you during the day that would mean the most to you?

RECOMMENDED READING:

Dr. Gary Chapman, *The Five Love Languages* (Chicago: Northfield Publishers, 1995).

CHAPTER 5

MONEY MATTERS

♥   *We live in an age of persuasive advertising and of skillful salesmanship, all designed to entice us to spend. An extravagant husband or wife can jeopardize any marriage. I think it is a good principle that each have some freedom and independence with everyday, necessary expenditures, while at the same time always discussing and consulting and agreeing on large expenditures. There would be fewer rash decisions, fewer unwise investments, fewer consequent losses, fewer bankruptcies if husbands and wives would counsel together on such matters and seek counsel from others.*   ♥

—Teachings of Gordon B. Hinckley (*Salt Lake City: Deseret Book,* 1997), pp. 652–53

Unless you've been independent for a while before getting married, the cost of being a newlywed can come as quite a shock. Not only do you have a phone bill but you also have to pay for the phone to be installed. You have electricity, but you might have to pay a deposit and a fee to have service begin. You have a monthly rent payment, but you might also have to pay first and last month's rent and a security deposit. You used to be covered under Mom and Dad's insurance, but now you're on your own. Now you understand why Dad was always walking around the house saying, "Who left this light on?" or "Why is hot water running down the sink?" Life is expensive.

Money matters in a marriage, and carelessness with cash is one of the major causes of difficulty in marriage. Because of your gospel training, you know that money is not the most important thing in the world, but you also know that you need it to live. In the classic movie *It's a Wonderful Life*, the following exchange takes place between George Bailey and Clarence the angel:

> *George: You don't happen to have eight thousand bucks on you, do ya?*

*Clarence: Oh no, we don't use money
in heaven.*

George: Oh yeah, I keep forgettin.'
Comes in pretty handy down here, Bub.
It sure does.

YOU CAN'T BEGIN WHERE YOUR PARENTS ARE NOW

Ask the parents of newlyweds, and more than a few will tell you they started out with nothing. They might also tell you that their kids are a little impatient, and want to start out with all the things it has taken them decades to accumulate.

Part of marriage is relocating. It's a little ironic, but people usually start out marriage with brand-new china, silverware, and matching glassware in an old, worn-out basement apartment. For some, the adjustment isn't difficult, and they can turn any apartment into a home. Others may feel forever uncomfortable until they catch up with their parents' lifestyle. They see Mom and Dad and maybe some of their siblings with new cars and computers, living a Martinelli's lifestyle, and they may try to match it on a Kool-Aid income.

President N. Eldon Tanner gave some wonderful financial advice years ago in general conference. His five main points were: (1) pay an honest tithing, (2) live on less than you earn, (3) distinguish between needs and wants, (4) develop and live within a budget, and (5) be honest in all financial affairs (see *Ensign*, November 1979, pp. 81–82). Let's talk about each of those points.

Pay an Honest Tithe

We think it's significant that President Tanner would mention paying tithing first. It's not something to start doing "once you get established" or "if you have money left over." We don't pay tithing because we can afford to, but because we can't afford not to. It's part of wise financial planning right now, because it involves the generous blessings of the Lord. President Gordon B. Hinckley has taught:

> *Reporters who I have met simply cannot believe that we pay 10 percent of our income as tithing. I explain that this is a spiritual phenomenon. We pay because we*

are obedient to the commandment of the Lord. We pay because we have faith in His munificent promises. Let us teach our children while they are yet young of the great opportunity and responsibility of paying tithing. If we do so, there will be another generation, and yet another, who will walk in the ways of the Lord and merit His promised blessing. (Ensign, November 1997, p. 69)

Maybe you've had your own way of paying tithing in the past, but now would be a good time to decide how you will do it as a couple. Do you pay once a month? Whenever you get a check? At tithing settlement? Decide now, but be sure tithing is part of your plan. Obedience to the law of tithing will bless any marriage. Don't take our word for it; just read Malachi 3:8–12 and Doctrine and Covenants 64:23.

Live on Less Than You Earn

Calvin Coolidge said, "There is no dignity quite so impressive and no independence quite so important as living within your means." There are two ways to live on less than you earn: earn more or spend less. That's it. Financial management is really quite simple to understand, but not nearly as easy to do.

The world has made it possible for people to have more than they can afford through a thing called *credit*. We'll open that can of worms later. But for now, we'll just say that we think one of the greatest principles to understand and implement as newlyweds is that of delaying gratification. "Delaying gratification" means to sacrifice something now for some reward or goal you desire later.

You've probably seen this sign near the handle of several refrigerators: "Nothing tastes as good as being thin feels." The dietary theory is to keep your mind on the lasting feeling of being thin, not on the temporary taste of chocolate. A financial counterpart to this saying would read something like this: "No new furniture, appliance, or electronic gadget brings as much pleasure as the feeling of being debt free." Being debt free is a great peace-of-mind type feeling. In fact, a common phrase used to describe a euphoric feeling is, "It's like having money in the bank."

Of course, there are certain things for which debt

may be necessary. If that's the case for you, pay off your debts before buying too much more. That's delaying gratification. President Hinckley has taught:

> *Debt can be a terrible thing. It is so easy to incur and so difficult to repay. Borrowed money is had only at a price, and that price can be burdensome. . . . I hasten to add that borrowing under some circumstances is necessary. Perhaps you need to borrow to complete your education. If you do, see that you pay it back. And do so promptly even at the sacrifice of some comforts that you might otherwise enjoy. You likely will have to borrow in securing a home. But be wise and do not go beyond your ability to pay.* (Teachings of Gordon B. Hinckley, p. 154)

Distinguish Between Needs and Wants

Someone once said, "Just as soon as people make enough money to live comfortably, they want to live extravagantly." Today, things that used to be "wants" are quickly becoming "needs." A personal computer is a good example; it may well be a need, but the question to ask is what kind of personal computer is needed? Does it have to be the best, or could you get by with a cheaper model? This applies to everything: cars, apartments, even groceries. Sometimes the extra money you pay is simply for the luxury of the brand name. For the most part, brand names are a want and not a need. (Brand-name clothes are okay if you don't mind paying the extra money for the right to be a walking billboard.)

We once heard some good advice about curbing unnecessary spending, and it has helped us in our lives. In fact, some people have even inserted a little card in their wallet with these three questions: "Do we need it? Do we need it now? Can we live without it?"

Develop and Live Within a Budget

A budget is the "spiritual creation" of your financial life that precedes the "physical creation." Jesus taught, "For which of you, intending to build a tower, sitteth not down first, and counteth the cost, whether he have sufficient to finish it?" (Luke 14:28). A budget is nothing more than sitting down and counting the cost.

Lots of people spend pretty haphazardly. They

scratch their heads at the end of the month and wonder where all the money went. Roger W. Babson said, "More people should learn to tell their dollars where to go instead of asking them where they went." Budgeting is telling the dollars where to go.

When we developed our budget, we first looked at our monthly income. Then we noted what fixed amounts we knew we had to pay out each month, like tithing, rent, health insurance, and car insurance. On the variable expenses—electric bill, fuel bill, gasoline, food—we had to guess. That's why it's a good idea to keep records of what you spend each month so that you can project what your future expenditures will be. The critical thing (and the obvious thing) is that your income should be greater than your outgo. If not, find a way to either make more or spend less.

Don't be overly shy about being a mooch. It's a great blessing to have parents who give you a bag of groceries or send you a check once in a while. It's humbling, but let your parents bless you when they offer. That's what families are for. "And he who feeds you, or clothes you, or gives you money, shall in nowise lose his reward" (D&C 84:90).

Of course, it's also wise to save something each month—preferably in a savings account or money market account where it's not at risk. It's not a good idea to put money at risk if you don't have much. One financial planner put his whole philosophy into two rules: (1) Live on less than you earn; (2) Don't lose what you save! Kin Hubbard said, "The safest way to double your money is to fold it over and put it in your pocket."

Budgeting means planning. And every plan has a desired result. It's amazing, but there are in this country people of retirement age who haven't saved anything, and who never had a plan. Now is the time to start saving. The sooner you start, the less you'll have to put away each month, and the greater will be the result.

Be Honest in All Your Financial Affairs

We don't think you need any commentary from us about being honest. There's one place where it's especially tempting to cheat a little, though, which is worth a mention. It's been said that all new money printed these days has a natural homing instinct to the IRS. Paying taxes is one of the great joys of life, and though you may not agree with the immensely complicated tax code, there's no justification for cheating. The eternal penalties of being dishonest with our fellowman far outweigh the temporary penalties imposed by the IRS.

YOU HAVE BEEN PREAPPROVED TO GIVE US YOUR MONEY!

Okay, here's a scary thought: As soon as it is known by the world that you are a newlywed, credit card companies will want to get you started—or should we say addicted to—spending money their way. Unfortunately, many couples can't resist the temptation to start out with new stuff, and they fall for the "buy now, pay later" pitch.

When you use credit, you are "renting" the money from the credit card company, and the rent is called interest. Maybe you've heard the old saying about interest: "Thems who understands it, collects it; thems who don't, pays it." President Gordon B. Hinckley spoke of his concern for the indebtedness of many people in the priesthood session of a recent general conference:

I am troubled by the huge consumer installment debt which hangs over the people of the nation, including our own people. In March 1997 that debt totaled $1.2 trillion, which represented a 7 percent increase over the previous year.

In December of 1997, 55 to 60 million households in the United States carried credit card balances. These balances averaged more than $7,000 and cost $1,000 per year in interest and fees. Consumer debt as a percentage of disposable income rose from 16.3 percent in 1993 to 19.3 percent in 1996.

Everyone knows that every dollar borrowed carries with it the penalty of paying interest. . . .

President J. Reuben Clark Jr., in the priesthood meeting of the conference in 1938, said from this pulpit: "Once in debt, interest is your companion every minute of every day and night; you cannot shun it or slip away from it; you cannot dismiss it; it yields neither to entreaties, demands, or orders; and whenever you get in its way or cross its course or fail to meet its demands, it crushes you" (in Conference Report, Apr. 1938, 103). (Ensign, November 1998, p. 53)

It's interesting that credit card commercials usually depict young couples on exotic vacations enjoying incredible freedom. The slogan is, "It's everywhere you want to be." Yeah, well, so's the interest, because you can't get away from it no matter how far you travel.

Credit is not always a bad thing. Most people will have to go into debt to finance certain long-term expenses like homes or education, but that's where it should stop if possible. Those things are usually referred to as *investment* debt. What we're talking about is *consumer* debt.

Try to avoid using a credit card for little things, because little things add up to big things, and that means a big monthly payment. Besides, most people who are deep in credit card debt have a hard time remembering what they bought in the first place! The credit card companies try to fool you with that "low minimum monthly payment," but don't be deceived. At as much as 24 percent interest that some companies charge, you could end up paying $15.72 for your Happy Meal by the time you actually get around to paying it off.

It takes a long time to pay off large credit card debt.

Bernard Poduska, an LDS marriage and family therapist and author of *For Love and Money*, wrote:

> In today's credit world, our primary concern is usually the size of the monthly payments. We then make payments on an outstanding balance for so long that we forget what exactly it was that we bought. We also lose sight of the actual cost of individual items, including taxes and interest charges, in the homogeneity of minimal payments. Then, as most of today's families simply add the newly acquired credit card payments (including interest) to their other monthly expenditures, the next month's money runs out even sooner than the last month's—and the credit cards get used even earlier in the month. Too often, this insidious progression continues until families see bankruptcy as the only way out. (For Love and Money [Salt Lake City: Deseret Book, 1995], pp. 177–78)

When Elder Jeffrey R. Holland was president of Brigham Young University, he and his wife, Patricia, spoke to the student body about a different kind of plastic surgery:

> PAT:. . . . Controlling your financial circumstances is another one of those "marriage skills"—and we put that in quotation marks—that obviously matters to everyone and matters long before entering into marriage. One of the great laws of heaven and earth is that your expenses need to be less than your income. You can reduce your anxiety and your pain and your early marital discord—indeed, you can reduce your parents' anxiety and pain and marital discord right now!—if you will learn to manage a budget.

> JEFF: As part of this general financial caution, we encourage, if necessary, plastic surgery for both husband and wife. This is a very painless operation, and it may give you more self-esteem than a new nose job or a tummy tuck. Just cut up your credit cards. Unless you are prepared to use those cards

under the strictest of conditions and restraints, you should not use them at all—at least not at 18 percent or 21 percent or 24 percent interest. No convenience known to modern man has so jeopardized the financial stability of a family—especially young strug-gling families—as has the ubiquitous credit card. "Don't leave home without it?" That's precisely why he is leaving home—

PAT:—*and why she is leaving him!*
(On Earth as It Is in Heaven [*Salt Lake City, Deseret Book, 1989*], *pp. 105–6*)

Of course, it's not a sin to have a credit card. They're handy for emergencies and for travel. But they have to be used carefully. And when the telemarketers call you (and as fresh young newlyweds with no credit history, you can rest assured, they will find you), it's really nice to be able to say, "No thanks, we don't have any consumer debt, we don't want any consumer debt, and we don't need any credit cards. Thank you." Besides, no new piece of furniture feels as comfortable as being debt free.

THE GHOST OF CHRISTMAS PRESENTS

As newlyweds, we had different backgrounds in gift giving that came to haunt our first holidays together. We came from families where the gift-giving traditions were quite different. Kim was the first one married in her family, and all of her siblings still lived at home. She traditionally gave more expensive gifts to each individual in the family, as there were relatively few to buy for. With five siblings, their spouses, and twenty-plus nieces and nephews, John's family had long ago decided to draw names rather than giving each person in the extended family a separate gift. We soon discovered that the Christmas budget and formula for gift giving was just as important as the budget for food and rent (though a little more emotionally charged).

BOTTOM LINE

As in every other area of your marriage, when it comes to money, the main thing is to communicate. Talk about and agree on your financial goals, and then make a commitment to be disciplined about spending limits.

(You might also try to set some "contention limits" over money problems.) We made several money decisions as newlyweds. We decided that it would take some time to have the things our folks had. We decided that our relationship was more important than keeping up with the Joneses. We also decided that we were more excited about earning interest than paying it. Most important, we decided that we would follow what we've been taught about money, always pay our tithing, and have faith in the Lord's promises.

ACTION STEPS

Determine what your income will be per month.

Determine what you spend each month.

Budget!

Set a goal for savings.

Discuss how money matters were handled in your home.

RECOMMENDED READING:

James Christensen, *Rich on Any Income* (Salt Lake City: Shadow Mountain, 1985)

Bernard Poduska, *For Love and Money* (Salt Lake City: Deseret Book, 1995)

CHAPTER 6

INTIMACY

♥   ♥

Let the husband render unto the wife due benevolence: and likewise also the wife unto the husband.

The wife hath not power of her own body, but the husband: and likewise also the husband hath not power of his own body, but the wife.

Defraud ye not one the other, except it be with consent for a time, that ye may give yourselves to fasting and prayer; and come together again, that Satan tempt you not for your incontinency.

—*1 Corinthians 7:3–5*

Needless to say, a temple marriage is an unforgettable experience. During the sealing ceremony, the Spirit soars as powerful words are spoken and the sealing power is administered. As you're surrounded by loving relatives and friends, your thoughts naturally turn to your present and future families, your "roots and branches," and the wonderful binding covenants pronounced upon you. Later, while you walk around the temple grounds to have pictures taken or to visit, the beautiful spirit of the temple remains.

Speaking for ourselves, once we were home from the honeymoon and back into a normal telestial routine, we reflected on how quickly something that had once been "no, no, no" became "go, go, go." Because LDS youth have all heard so many cautions about dating and chastity, some get the impression that sex is bad and unspeakable.

It's important to understand that these lessons are given not because sex is bad but precisely because it's so good. That's why the word *sacred* is often used to describe sexual intimacy. Our sexual nature was given to us by God, and the purpose of sexual intimacy is not just to bring children into the world but also to create loving bonds between husband and wife. President Spencer W. Kimball, in a general conference address, quoted the Reverend Billy Graham as saying:

> The Bible celebrates sex and its proper use, presenting it as God-created, God-ordained, God-blessed. It makes plain that God himself implanted the physical magnetism between the sexes for two reasons: for the propagation of the human race, and for the expression of that kind of love between man and wife that makes for true oneness. His command to the first man and woman to be "one flesh" was as important as his command to "be fruitful and multiply." (Reader's Digest, May 1970, p. 118, as cited in Ensign, May 1974, p. 7)

As you might have guessed, this chapter was difficult for us to write. Sure, this topic is very personal and not something that we normally discuss with friends, but that wasn't the hard part. The challenge was how to convey the sacredness of the topic in a world that cheapens sexual intimacy at every opportunity. Elder Jeffrey R. Holland gave an address titled "Of Souls, Symbols, and Sacraments" in which he spoke of the physical union of a married man and a woman as something so sacred it could be called a *sacrament*. He said:

> *Sexual intimacy is not only a symbolic union between a man and a woman—the uniting of their very souls—but it is also symbolic of a union between mortals and deity, between otherwise ordinary and fallible humans uniting for a rare and special moment with God himself and all the powers by which he gives life in this wide universe of ours.*
>
> *In this latter sense, human intimacy is a sacrament, a very special kind of symbol. . . .*
>
> *. . . Indeed, if our definition of sacrament is that act of claiming and sharing and exercising God's own inestimable power, then I know of virtually no other divine privilege so routinely given to us all—*

women or men, ordained or unordained, Latter-day Saint or non-Latter-day Saint— than the miraculous and majestic power of transmitting life, the unspeakable, unfathomable, unbroken power of procreation.

(On Earth as It Is in Heaven, *pp. 193–95*)

We hope that we can maintain this reverent spirit toward the sacrament of intimacy as we continue with this chapter.

HAPPY HONEYMOON!

We received lots of advice from many sources during our short engagement, and much of it was about what to expect on our honeymoon. Kim's dad gave us some wise counsel: "Just don't over-expect. Have fun together, and things will get better and more natural with time." That advice was very calming and helped us not to be overly nervous.

We'd also heard several one-liners like, "Men are like microwaves, and women are like crock-pots," and other things that we didn't completely understand at the time. Because we had tried to follow the inspired counsel given in all those standards nights we'd heard over the years, we went off to the bridal suite wonderfully naive.

One of the best pieces of pre-honeymoon advice we received was from an old friend who strongly recommended we read a book called *The Act of Marriage* by Tim and Beverly LaHaye. This book is thorough and specific, and was written in a reverent spirit by committed Christians. It handles specifics about anatomy and male and female response that we couldn't find in any other book we read. We read it together during the final weeks of our engagement. (We agreed not to make eye contact while reading because of our frequent blushing.) We have since recommended it to many of our newlywed friends and highly recommend it to you too.

Just as with every other aspect of marriage we've discussed so far, it's important to talk about your expectations. Some couples—probably more couples than any of us realize—have a rather frustrating time on their honeymoon. After the wedding night, many have expressed the thought, "Is *that* what all the fuss is about? You can get excommunicated for *that?*" Many couples aren't even intimate the first night because they're so thoroughly exhausted from the wedding day and reception! But there's no need to worry; they'll have plenty of time later. (We're married for eternity, right?)

In your intimate relationship, just like in everything else in your marriage, the things you want to accomplish together will take time, understanding, and effort. So be patient, and don't be alarmed or think your marriage is doomed if the honeymoon is frustrating. Focus on the wonderful opportunity to be off by yourselves as you begin your new life. We think the best part of our honeymoon was just being able to snuggle up together with the realization that we'd never have to say good-bye at the doorstep again.

ROMANCE BEGINS AT BREAKFAST

For those first few days after your wedding, the pressures of school and work are left behind. It's a wonderful time to forget about the world and just get to know one another. Once you're back home, absorbed in the complicated pursuits of life, you have to find time to re-create the honeymoon magic. One of the things we learned is that intimacy is not just a physical thing, although we often use the word to mean just that. The sexual aspect of intimacy is only a small part of the experience, especially for women. There is also sharing and talking and closeness that is emotional as well as physical. G. Hugh Allred, a professional counselor, has observed:

> The foundation of [sexual] relationship[s] is good relations between husband and wife in all other areas. It is difficult for a wife to give of herself spontaneously and freely if she is resentful and angry with her husband. Both must work to be respectful, courteous, loving with each other in all areas of their interaction so that they can give freely and without fear of being hurt in this most intimate of relationships. . . . Both man and wife should be sensitive to those things that impede good sexual relationships. Unproductive and unresolved conflict; lack of privacy; fear of being ridiculed, hurt, dominated, or used; fear of losing oneself to another; fatigue; in-law problems; business difficulties; and lack of confidence in oneself

> or one's mate are among those things that
> most often hinder good sexual relationships.
> (How to Strengthen Your Marriage and
> Family [Provo: Brigham Young University
> Press, 1976], p. 255)

It may be that the most romantic thing a husband can do for his wife is the dishes! When she feels secure and loved and cherished, it is easier for her to feel romantic. By the same token, when the husband feels admired and respected by his wife, he is more likely to want to express his love. So let the romance begin at breakfast! If doing the dishes doesn't work, spend some time talking with one another. Dr. Brent A. Barlow shares this experience:

> Dr. Lynn Scoresby once visited one of
> my classes for newlyweds at BYU as a guest
> lecturer on sexual relationships in marriage.
> One student asked him if there were any
> true aphrodisiacs (something that arouses
> sexual interest). He said, "Yes, prolonged
> conversation." He said that simple conver-
> sation between husband and wife for an

extended period of time literally puts them in
sync with each other and prepares them
for more intimate interaction. (Just for
Newlyweds [*Salt Lake City: Deseret Book,*
1992], p. 50)

Conversation, eh? Hmmm. That ought to motivate
men to talk and listen more often.

COMMUNICATE

Originally, we were going to call this chapter "A Few
Words about Intimacy." We thought that would fit nicely,
since we were just too darn embarrassed to write a lot of
words about intimacy. After a few years of marriage, we're
still a little shy. Latter-day Saints are generally not very
used to talking about intimacy in public, and that's probably a good thing. But it's okay to talk about these things
with your spouse. (If it still feels uncomfortable, hold
your marriage certificate in your lap while you talk.)
Many couples are frustrated sexually but unwilling to
share with their spouse what they want. So to help get
the conversation started, we're going to turn to Dr. Brent
Barlow to supply the Action Steps for this chapter with

some discussion questions from his book *Just for Newlyweds:*

ACTION STEPS

1. Agree to talk often and openly about your sexual relationship. Seek to help each other attain intimacy in your marriage. If both of you are aware of the dynamics involved in giving and receiving, you will find that the more you give, the more you get is the general rule. Make a good sex life in your marriage a high priority for both of you.

2. Realize that intimacy can exist apart from sexual relationships, and seek intimacy in other ways such as communication, joint activities, and spiritual endeavors.

3. Take time, or arrange times, for intimacy and sexual fulfillment. This is critical in contemporary marriage because of more hectic schedules resulting, in part, from an increasing number of wives in the work force.

4. Read 1 Corinthians 7:2–5 often. What are the implications of verse five for newlyweds?

5. Focus on the total marital relationship. Remember that sex is an extension of the relationship and not the relationship

itself. Work to improve other areas of your marriage along with the sexual dimension.

6. Remember the first two qualities of Christ-like love mentioned in the scriptures: "Charity suffereth long [is patient], and is kind." (1 Cor. 13:4; Moro. 7:45.) This is particularly true in the sexual relationships in marriage.

7. Understand that sex serves several functions in a marriage, including relationship enhancement, reproduction, personal fulfillment, communication, pleasure, spiritual development, and, on occasion, tension release.

8. Sexual fulfillment probably results from 90 percent attitude and 10 percent skills.

9. What we don't know can hurt us. Seek to eliminate misunderstandings about sex, especially those perpetuated by the media. When necessary, study and learn from appropriate sources about the sexual area of marriage.

10. Focus on your success in regard to your sexual relationship rather than on your failures. Remember that compliments bring far better results than complaints.

11. On occasion, allow for some variation, within propriety, in some aspects of your sexual relationship. Break the routines. Something as simple as changing time and place of sexual

interaction can help greatly. Routine sexual relationships, with little or no variation in either circumstances or conditions, may be deadly to your relationship. (Barlow, *Just for Newlyweds*, pp. 58–59.)

RECOMMENDED READING:

Tim and Beverly LaHaye, *The Act of Marriage: The Beauty of Sexual Love* (Grand Rapids, MI: Zondervan, 1998 ed.)

♥ ♥

CHAPTER 7

KEEPING THE ROMANCE ALIVE

♥　　　　　　　　　　　　　　　　　　　♥

I think [the Lord] smiles when he sees young husbands and wives, and older ones, with deep affection for each other, who continue their courtship as our prophet has said, who continue to love each other with all their souls until the day they die and then accentuate it through eternity.

—*Spencer W. Kimball, in* I Know That My Reedemer Lives *(Salt Lake City: Deseret Book, 1990), p. 186*

When we were dating, we used to observe married people in their cars while waiting at traffic lights. Some of them stared straight ahead and never opened their mouths. They looked comatose! It appeared that the most excitement they had was the special thrill of watching the light change from red to green. Or maybe it was the gentle yet constant teek-oo, teek-oo, teek-oo of the turn signal that kept them from talking.

So what is the magic ingredient that ensures that newlyweds don't have to go out into traffic for excitement? Two words: *continual romance*. Most of the newlywed couples we know are determined to keep the romance alive, so their problem is not a lack of desire. They just find it a little more difficult with their new "Ramen noodle" budget, work schedules, and time-consuming college syllabi. And some young couples expect the romance to continue automatically, with little effort on their part. It doesn't happen that way!

COUPLE HOME EVENING

Keeping the romance alive requires spending time together, but it doesn't have to be expensive. That's a good thing, because newlywed budgets are typically tighter than dating budgets. So how do you keep that spark of romance in your marriage? Well, *it's about time* (double meaning intended). We once saw this equation on a Sunday School blackboard: "Shared Time + Shared Experiences = Intimacy." In this marital arithmetic, no mention is made of money or exotic travel; just doing things together creates friendship. Dr. Brent Barlow shares comments from several wives:

> [One] young woman said, "In the future, I would appreciate more planning for time together. Specifically, setting aside time for just us. Time to share experiences, develop interests we can share, become better acquainted, and just be good friends."

> An older woman wished her husband would just "offer to go out in the evening for a walk or bike ride."

> Wives do expect an occasional night out with their husbands. One happy wife said, "I enjoy going on little trips with him or just a date to dinner or a show. But it doesn't have to cost anything to make me happy. All he has to do is let me know he's glad I'm there." And another satisfied housewife

*simply wrote, "We have a regular date
night. He tries very hard to follow the advice
of our church leaders, who say we should go
out alone as husband and wife."*

*Some wives don't want to go out on the
spur of the moment. One wife admonished
husbands, "Plan ahead for dates. Spur of
the moment planning is difficult, and by
planning you can get more in. Or, it can
just make you happier in looking forward to
the time together."* (What Wives Expect
of Husbands *[Salt Lake City: Deseret
Book, 1982], p. 124)*

Newlyweds are expected to hold family home
evening. In addition, Church leaders have counseled
husbands and wives to have a "date" once a week. We're
not sure if this is official Church policy, but many couples
we know consider Friday night their don't-you-dare-
make-an-appointment date night. We call it "couple
home evening," although it doesn't have to be spent at
home.

INEXPENSIVE DATING IDEAS

We've worked hard to keep the romance alive in our marriage, and we thought you might benefit from a few of our ideas. They may not be your style, but we thought it might help get your creativity going so you can come up with your own ideas. Please forgive the personal experiences (we have to use personal experiences about us because we don't know any personal experiences about you).

Kim Says:

On Valentine's Day, John had me go upstairs to get ready for the evening. He told me to stay upstairs until he came to "pick me up." At 7:00 he arrived upstairs with a blindfold in his hand. He put it on me and gently led me down the stairs. As I concentrated on not tripping down the stairs in my high heels, I also noticed the sound of birds singing in the background over a babbling brook. (John has a tape of nature sounds.) He pulled off the blindfold, and there I was standing in a forested picnic area in the middle of the living room. John had taken all of our houseplants and plastic ficus trees and made a secluded space on the living-room floor. On the floor were a red-checkered table-cloth (which he had purchased at the fabric store *all by himself*)

and a picnic basket. He thought of everything, right down to the goblets to go with the sparkling grape juice. It was one of the most romantic (and inexpensive) dates we have been on.

John Says:

Here's something Kim did for me. One night after working hard, I came home to a big sign on the garage door that read, "There's no place like home." Kim had decorated it with a rainbow and a yellow brick road. When I opened the door, there was a pair of red socks with a note that said, "Put on the ruby red slippers." Along the floor through our kitchen all the way to our room were yellow bricks leading the way, and notes about the scarecrow, tin man, and lion. At our door, another note read, "Click your heels together three times and say, 'There's no wife like Kim.' " As I did as I was told, I heard from inside, "You may enter." Kim had replaced all our lightbulbs with green ones, had covered our bed with a green sheet, brought in our green towels and rugs from the bathroom, and draped everything else with green cellophane. There she sat under a sign that read, "Welcome to Oz." "Oh, Auntie Em," I said to myself as I clicked my red socks together, "there's no place like home."

Kim Says:

After only three weeks of marriage, we went to California

together with my family for a cousin's wedding. We went to Disneyland, where John hadn't been since he was a small child. He had to leave early, so I stayed with my family for another few days before joining him again in Provo. My family dropped me off, and when I walked in the door, there was a big picture of Mickey and Minnie Mouse holding a sign that read "Welcome to Loverland." Along with the candles that lined my pathway, there were secret notes, along with a code to decipher each little message, just like on the "Indiana Jones" ride at Disneyland. A few steps up was a bottle of Martinelli's sparkling cider, and a few steps away from that was a box of chocolates. All the while I had to decipher each little message before I could get the biggest gift of all—a wonderful reunion with my husband after being separated.

John Says:

Here's a cosmic experience Kim arranged for me. I had often told her that it would be fun to buy some of those glow-in-the-dark stars and put them all over our ceiling, but we never really got around to doing it. One night after coming home from a two-day visit to Idaho, I met Kim in our room. She told me to come over and lie on my back on the bed. Then she handed me a card that said, "You are invited . . . to an evening under the stars." No sooner had I read those words than she flipped off the lights, revealing the heavenly glow from her hours and hours of work plastering stars all over our ceiling. Now we get a star show every night. (And if the adhesive ever wears out, we'll watch falling stars.)

What these dates have in common, besides being relatively inexpensive, is that they required time and planning on someone's part. Once again, it's about time. When you see that your spouse has gone to all that trouble for you, well . . . *that's* romantic.

GIFTS OF THE HEART

When we don't have much money, we give each other "gifts of the heart." That's not a cop-out. World-class gift givers know that "gifts of the heart" are the best even if they *can* afford something else. Many a wife would rather go on a walk with her husband for the evening than have him say, "Here's a dozen long-stemmed roses and some jewelry—enjoy those while I watch Monday Night Football."

Kim Says:

Some of these ideas require a little extra planning, but it is

amazing what your brain can come up with when your budget is tight. One Valentine's Day, John's gift to me was a simple piece of day-planner paper that has meant much more to me than the one cent it cost him to make. Typed across the top were the words: "Sixty seconds to happiness. Whenever you need a pick-me-up, just read this little card and it will make you happy." Below he had written sixty specific things that he loved about me, from the way I talk with my hands right down to my singing in the shower. It fit right into my planner, and I carry it with me always. It is a constant reminder of how much my husband cares for me. And last year for Christmas he gave me a "better husband," with a series of gifts and letters explaining all the things he would try to improve on to make our marriage better. That was the best gift of all.

IF YOU DON'T DATE, IT'S THE PITS

We try to alternate who plans the date night. That way we learn each other's definition of what a fun date is. The main thing is to arrange time to do things together. We had a relatively short engagement and courtship, so one of the things we decided after we got married was that we should still go out on a lot of dates.

Marriage becomes dull only if you let it. And we don't think you really need much help with creativity. There are millions of ideas out there. We also think that everyone has expert help available on how to be romantic. Just ask your spouse!

ACTION STEPS

Make a commitment to have a weekly date night.

Ask about your partner's ideal romantic date.

Plan a date for this weekend.

RECOMMENDED READING:

Blair Tolman, compiler, *Dating for Under a Dollar: 301 Ideas* (Salt Lake City: Granite Publishing, 1995)

Tomima Edmark, *365 Ways to Date Your Love: A Daily Guide to Creative Romance* (Fort Worth, Texas: Summit Publishing Group, 1995)

Barbara and Michael Jonas, *The Book of Love, Laughter & Romance* (San Francisco: Games Partnership Limited, Inc., 1994)

CHAPTER 8

KEEPING CHRIST IN YOUR MARRIAGE

♥ ─────────────────────── ♥

No divorce ever comes where there is in the hearts of hus-
band and wife, the pure love of Christ, for that love is based in
righteousness, and righteousness is an enemy of sin.

—*Joseph Fielding Smith*, The Restoration of All Things

(*Salt Lake City: Deseret Book, 1945*), *p. 239*

Why do we have the gospel, and what is the Church
for? Why is temple marriage so important? Why would
the Church issue a Proclamation to the World about

families? What is all this about, anyway? Elder Bruce R. McConkie offered this answer:

> *From the moment of birth into mortality to the time we are married in the temple, everything we have in the whole gospel system is to prepare and qualify us to enter that holy order of matrimony which makes us husband and wife in this life and in the world to come.*
>
> *Then from the moment we are sealed together by the power and authority of the holy priesthood—the power to bind on earth and have it sealed eternally in the heavens—from that moment everything connected with revealed religion is designed to help us keep the terms and conditions of our marriage covenant, so that this covenant will have efficacy, virtue, and force in the life to come.*
>
> *Thus celestial marriage is the crowning ordinance of the gospel, the crowning ordinance of the house of the Lord. Thus the*

> *family unit is the most important organiza-*
> *tion in time or in eternity.* (Improvement
> Era, *June 1970, p. 43)*

If this is true (and it is), then it makes sense to suppose that the adversary would do everything in his power
to frustrate the development of marriages and families.
One of the most sobering quotes we've heard came from
President Harold B. Lee back in 1972: "Satan's greatest
threat today is to destroy the family, and to make mockery of the law of chastity and the sanctity of the marriage
covenant" (*Church News*, 19 August 1972, p. 3). This
quote becomes especially scary if you personalize it:
Satan's greatest threat today is to destroy *your* family, and
make a mockery of the sanctity of *your* marriage
covenant. Obviously, this statement is prophetic, as evi-
denced by the efforts we see all around us to redefine and
erode the family.

Fortunately, there is also a holy power available to
bless our families. President Howard W. Hunter told the
story of Jairus, a ruler in the synagogue who approached
Jesus and said, "My little daughter lieth at the point of
death: I pray thee, come and lay thy hands on her, that

she may be healed; and she shall live" (Mark 5:23). Then President Hunter observed, "These are not only the words of faith of a father torn with grief but are also a reminder to us that whatever Jesus lays his hands upon lives. If Jesus lays his hands upon a marriage, it lives. If he is allowed to lay his hands on the family, it lives" (*Ensign*, November 1979, p. 65).

So that's the way it is. Satan wants to destroy your marriage, but if the Savior will lay his hands on your marriage, it will live. How do you do that? How can you get the Savior to touch your marriage?

Maybe you are acquainted with the famous painting that shows Jesus standing outside a door knocking and waiting. This depiction of Revelation 3:20 is a wonderful illustration of agency. The door is shown without a handle, because it must be opened from the inside. If you want the Savior to touch your marriage, he must be invited to do so. He is eager to be allowed inside—he stands at the door and knocks!—but he will not force himself in.

So how do you invite him in? We've found that one of the greatest joys of married life is praying together, studying scriptures together, and attending the temple together. These things, when done consistently, allow Christ inside to bless our marriage. These practices are critical in the first year of marriage (and vital for all the years that follow) for a couple of reasons. First of all, you begin a pattern for the rest of your marriage. Second, it's much harder to feel resentment or unkind feelings toward your spouse when you're on your knees together at the end of the day. It's wonderful to be able to thank your Father in Heaven for your spouse and express your love for your partner when he or she is kneeling beside you.

President Gordon B. Hinckley has taught:

> If there be any among you who are not having family prayer, let that practice start now, to get on your knees together, if you can possibly do it, every morning and every evening, and speak to the Lord and express your thanks, invoke His blessings upon the needy of the earth, and speak to Him concerning your own well-being. I believe that God our Eternal Father will hear our prayers, and I urge you to have family

prayers. (Teachings of Gordon B. Hinckley [*Salt Lake City: Deseret Book,* 1997], p. 217)

We also try to have spiritual experiences together. We like to attend firesides, take adult religion classes, and deliver dinners to those who need them. We want to grow *together*, and that includes growing spiritually. Elder Neal A. Maxwell wrote, "In the living Church it is vital that husbands and wives grow together in their gospel scholarship and in their Christian service. We do not want our men to be the theologians and our women the Christians. The living Church encourages symmetry, not separateness" (*Things As They Really Are* [Salt Lake City: Deseret Book, 1978], p. 58).

President Boyd K. Packer taught (read this one slowly): "True doctrine, understood, changes attitudes and behavior. The study of the doctrines of the gospel will improve behavior quicker than a study of behavior will improve behavior" (*Conference Report*, October 1986, p. 20). If you were to apply that principle to your marriage, the quote might read like this: "The study of the doctrines of the gospel will improve a marriage quicker than a study of marriage will improve a marriage." This is why we have placed a high priority on studying and learning the gospel together.

COMMUNICATION OR CHRISTLIKE ATTRIBUTES?

The world's expertise would tell you that most marriage problems would be solved if couples could learn improved communication. But is that really the case? Dr. Douglas E. Brinley, an LDS marriage counselor, produced an audio seminar in which he contrasted the world's approach with the gospel approach. In it, he maintains that he doesn't remember ever having heard a general conference talk on communication or listening skills. Those topics don't show up in the scriptures very often either. He says:

> Now, that's interesting to me, because
> what happens is . . . when a couple comes
> in to see you, you notice rather quickly that
> they don't communicate with each other
> very well . . . so you begin to think that the
> problem is that they don't know how to

communicate. Then you learn an interesting thing: that you communicate with them quite well. I think I understand what he's mad about; I think I understand what she'd like him to do differently, so [I can see] that I communicate fairly well with them. I notice that he communicates pretty well with the secretary at the office. . . . And they are glad she's teaching Relief Society, and I don't hear people say, "Run that by me again, I'm not getting that."

So what I've come to decide is, that the Brethren are right, that this [Christlike attributes] is where the problem is, not over here [communication skills]. . . .

How much money do you think a counselor would make if, after listening to a couple rip on each other, the counselor said, "You know, you two are probably the most un-Christlike people I've ever met. You're extremely rude and irrational to each other; you're probably upper-telestial at best. I think the Lord's pretty disappointed in what he sees in you two—in fact, I'm sure he's disappointed in the way you two are functioning. Why don't you grow up and act like adults, and realize that it takes mature people to make these things work."

Now, what do you suppose would happen about that point? Well, you wouldn't make a whole lot of money, 'cause there wouldn't be anybody left to counsel. Where do you think people want you to tell them the problem is? Right—with the partner they brought in to get fixed, or there's some communication skill that they've never learned, and if you could do that little quirk, just get that little twist, why, that would solve all the problems. (Marital Relationships Seminar, *Cassette 1, Side A [Salt Lake City: Covenant Communications, 1988])*

All the communication skills in the world will not help us unless we're striving to incorporate Christlike attributes. We agree with Brother Brinley, that people already know how to listen, and all of us are fairly competent at communicating our feelings when given a chance. What spouses need is the *willingness* to listen, and the *willingness* to talk. We need the change of heart that only the Savior can bring. Real, lasting change comes only from the Lord. We need patience, gentleness, meekness, love unfeigned, brotherly kindness, and so on. Then, all those communication skills have value.

Quoting Brother Brinley once more, "Without such theological perspectives, however, secular exercises designed to improve our relationship and our communication skills (the common tools of counselors and marriage books) will never work any permanent change in one's heart: *they simply develop more clever and skilled fighters!*" (*Toward a Celestial Marriage* [Salt Lake City: Bookcraft, 1986], p. 7).

IS MY SPOUSE MY NEIGHBOR?

As a child, you probably heard your parents say, "You treat your friends better than you treat your own family!" And in some instances, those parents were probably right. Hopefully, none of us will ever get to the point where we treat our neighbors better than our own spouses. Jesus set some fairly high standards on how we should treat our neighbors. Wouldn't your spouse qualify as even more important to you than the "neighbor" spoken of in the parable of the good Samaritan?

Is it possible that in the early years of marriage spouses may spend so much time together and get so used to each other that their manners expire? Once you're out of the temple, your partner has to stick with you, right? So you can relax a little—or so many people seem to think. Perhaps one of the temptations of the first year of marriage is to become complacent.

Alma the Elder explained that part of the baptismal covenant is to "bear one another's burdens, that they may be light." He also asked the baptismal candidates if they would be willing to "mourn with those that mourn; yea, and comfort those that stand in need of comfort" (Mosiah 18:8–9). Well, you can bear your spouse's burdens that they may be light. You can mourn with your spouse at times and give him or her comfort.

The Apostle Paul said, "Rejoice with them that do rejoice, and weep with them that weep" (Romans 12:15).

Notice that Paul didn't say, "Suggest solutions to those that weep, or tell them they cry too much and have no good reason to weep."

Whenever we overhear spouses being rude or unkind to each other, we wonder if they missed that lesson in Sunday School, or if they think all these admonitions apply only to people in the neighborhood but not to the person they made a solemn covenant with in the temple.

COVENANTS AND COMMITMENT ARE MORE CONSTANT THAN CHEMISTRY

If you are committed to your spouse the way the Savior was and is committed to the Church, your marriage will prosper. Paul wrote to the Ephesians, "Husbands, love your wives, even as Christ also loved the church, and gave himself for it" (Ephesians 5:25).

Some engaged couples believe that because they're getting married, they're at the end of their troubles. One young lady expressed this feeling to her mother, who responded, "Yes, but which end?" Or some newlyweds expect their spouses to make them happy. They may believe that because they've finally tied the knot, they'll never feel lonely or sad again. We even hear of marriages breaking up because a husband or wife "just isn't happy anymore." Author Karen Lynn Davidson has written, "I have yet to see marriage, by itself, turn an unhappy person into a happy person. A really happy married person is almost always one who was or could have been happy as a single person" (*Thriving On Our Differences* [Salt Lake City: Deseret Book, 1990], p. 39).

Every marriage has problems and perhaps a few hard times, especially in the first year. But don't give up! In our marriage, we've noticed that those "in-love" feelings aren't constant, but they return if *we* are constant. You may not feel the giddy, giggly, in-love feelings every day. That's okay. Real love has more to do with come-what-may commitment than anxiously engaged euphoria. You kiss and make up after a disagreement not just because you love your spouse but because you've made a *covenant* to love your spouse. Sure, love is a feeling, but it's also a choice, a commitment, and a covenant.

We still have a few of those "I need to talk" episodes once in a while, and we expect we'll have more. But the nice thing is that we *want* to work things out. Those heart-to-heart talks are successful not because we've been trained in communication skills but because we've made a covenant to be meek and teachable and humble, and we've made a covenant to stay with each other through thick and thin.

Years ago, the Church produced a public service announcement that said, "Marriage isn't any big thing, it's a lot of little things." We've always liked that. Little things are the most fun part of being married. It's true that acts of kindness every day create a happy marriage. Elder Bruce C. Hafen has written:

> *Having interpreted and reinterpreted the nuances of the law of Moses for centuries, most Jews were quite unprepared for the broad and lofty principles Jesus taught them. When the lawyer asked Jesus, "Which is the great commandment in the law?" he probably expected a complex answer. But the Lord told him simply, "Thou shalt love the Lord thy God with all thy heart, and with all thy soul, and with all thy mind. This is the first and great commandment. And the second is*

like unto it, Thou shalt love thy neighbour as thyself. On these two commandments hang all the law and the prophets." (Matthew 22:37–40.)

The gospel of the higher law was so simple and so profound that the Pharisees and other learned people of Christ's day missed it completely. They missed the simple part—the core—and they missed everything. (The Broken Heart [Salt Lake City: Deseret Book, 1989], p. 158)

Perhaps we could say that it's possible to miss the simple part and the core of marriage as well. Notice the first three words of these two commandments mentioned: "Thou shalt love . . ." It's interesting that when Jesus summarized all the law and the prophets, it came down to two phrases that both began with "Thou shalt love . . ." We think that these three words of Jesus are the great commandment in marriage too. Thou shalt love the Lord, and thou shalt love thy spouse.

Some may respond, "But sometimes I don't *feel* love. It seems to come and go." That may be true. When you're dating, love is a feeling. But when you're married, love becomes an action word; it's not only a noun, it's a verb! If you want to feel the love feeling again, don't sit around waiting for the "feeling" to come over you—get up and take some action. Love and serve your spouse!

FORGIVE AND FORGET

The Lord has said, "Behold, he who has repented of his sins, the same is forgiven, and I, the Lord, remember them no more" (D&C 58:42). There will be many times when you'll need to ask your spouse for forgiveness. It's inevitable. You will both make mistakes. But if you're truly committed to following the Lord, you'll not only forgive but you'll forget. Some spouses keep mental 3 x 5 cards in their head and remember each little offense. Then, when some new problem arises, they open the file box, bring out the 3 x 5 cards, and review each card, reminding their spouse of all his or her past offenses.

When your partner asks for forgiveness, and you offer that forgiveness, the incident should also be forgotten. Forgiveness without forgetting isn't really forgiveness—it's more like "marital probation." If the Lord will remember our sins no more, shouldn't we do the same for our spouses? That is the pattern the Lord has set for us.

A TEMPLE RECOMMENDATION

One of the best ways to have the Savior touch your marriage is to visit the temple. In those peaceful surroundings we remember our wedding day and the covenants we made. We've noticed that we sit apart throughout the endowment until we're reunited in the celestial room. It reminds us that we can be reunited someday in the place that room represents. We leave the temple with a renewed commitment to keep our covenants and keep the Spirit of the Lord in our marriage.

We're not content to just hope that our marriage will work. We're not leaving it up to chance. We're determined to make it work. And because we've been to the temple and been sealed, we believe the Lord is determined to help our covenant succeed as well.

Many years ago, President Spencer W. Kimball recommended that every LDS family have a particular picture on the wall:

It seems to me it would be a fine thing if every set of parents would have in every bedroom in their house a picture of the temple so the boy or girl from the time he is an infant could look at the picture every day and it becomes a part of his life. When he reaches the age that he needs to make this very important decision, it will have already been made. (The Teachings of Spencer W. Kimball, *ed. Edward L. Kimball [Salt Lake City: Bookcraft, 1982], p. 301*)

♥   ♥

We have already been through the temple, but we keep a picture of the temple for a different reason. We want it there to remind us of our covenants, and to remind us to return again. Temple attendance is our favorite way to keep Christ in our marriage.

FROM HERE TO ETERNITY

We have really enjoyed writing this book together. In fact, it's been really good for our marriage. We've had a lot of fun reliving our first year, remembering all the things we've done together and the challenges we've overcome. An unexpected side effect is that it has helped us grow closer than ever before. We hope it's been helpful for you too. We think every couple out there in newly-wed land should get started on their own marriage memory book.

We also hope this is just the beginning. One book on marriage can't possibly prepare you for all the challenges you may encounter. Fortunately, there are many wonderful gospel-centered books out there on marriage. There are many marriage workshops and firesides and *Ensign* articles available as well. Most important, the Lord is eager to help you make your marriage celestial.

A "temple marriage" indicates a location, but a "celestial marriage" indicates a quality. Your marriage may have been performed in the temple, but only the Lord can make it celestial. The greatest thing you can do for your marriage is be committed to the Lord and his gospel. It's not just about having an eternal perspective or remembering the plan of salvation. The plan of salvation *is* your marriage. It's your *personal* plan of salvation. Your exaltation is impossible without it. That's why it deserves so much attention and continued effort.

We're encouraged by this quotation from President Spencer W. Kimball: "While marriage is difficult, and discordant and frustrated marriages are common, yet real, lasting happiness is possible, and marriage can be more an exultant ecstasy than the human mind can conceive" (*Teachings of Spencer W. Kimball*, pp. 305–6). President James E. Faust expressed a similar feeling this way: "Happiness in marriage and parenthood can exceed a thousand times any other happiness" (*Ensign*, November 1977, p. 11).

This concludes a few ideas we wish we'd known when we were newlyweds. We hope you've enjoyed them. As you know, the wedding requires weeks of planning, but weddings are over in a day. Marriages, on the other hand, are intended to last forever, and they take a lot more time. They are the result of talking and planning and working. We love being married. To keep our marriage strong, we talk about it all the time. Mostly, we honor marriage as part of the Lord's plan, and ask the Lord to touch our marriage so it will live and grow. Best wishes to you in your first year, and we hope you live happily ever after, one day at a time.

ACTION STEPS

Discuss goals for scripture study, family prayer, and temple attendance.

Get another marriage book!

Discuss how gospel principles can help you have a better marriage.

INDEX